Working the Rock

Newfoundland and Labrador in the Photographs
of Edith S. Watson, 1890–1930

Frances Rooney

Library and Archives Canada Cataloguing in Publication

Rooney, Frances, author
      Working the Rock : Newfoundland and Labrador in the photographs of Edith S. Watson, 1890-1930 / Frances Rooney.

ISBN 978-1-927099-74-2 (softcover)

      1. Watson, Edith S., 1861-1943. 2. Watson, Edith S., 1861-1943--Travel--Newfoundland and Labrador. 3. Newfoundland and Labrador--Pictorial works. 4. Newfoundland and Labrador--History--Pictorial works. I. Title.

FC2162.R66 2017   971.8022'2   C2017-901606-7

© 2017 Frances Rooney

Contact the author at frooney2002@yahoo.com

Design and layout: John Andrews
Editor: Stephanie Porter
Copy editor: Iona Bulgin

Printed in Canada

Excerpts from this publication may be reproduced under licence from Access Copyright, or with the express written permission of Boulder Publications Ltd., or as permitted by law. All rights are otherwise reserved and no part of this publications may be reproduced, stored in a retrieval system, or transmitted in any form or by any means, electronic, mechanical, photocopying, scanning, recording, or otherwise, except as specifically authorized.

We acknowledge the financial support of the Government of Newfoundland and Labrador through the Department of Tourism, Culture and Recreation.

Funded by the Government of Canada | Financé par le gouvernement du Canada

Contents

About the Photographs 5

Finding Edith 7

"Edith Watson, Camera Artist" 21

Edith's Newfoundland and Labrador 61

Photography and the Photographs 105

Selected Bibliography 120

Acknowledgements 125

About the Author 127

Lois Foster Watson

January 6, 1916–August 20, 2014

About the Photographs

Most photographs here were taken by Edith S. Watson in Newfoundland and Labrador, c. 1891–1930, and come from the albums she compiled in the 1930s. The majority of captions are Edith's own, as they appear with the photographs (place names have been silently corrected). Captions *in italics* are by the author. Photographs from other sources are credited with the photo.

Each photograph has been processed without additional manipulation so as to preserve its original character, including flaws, as faithfully as possible. All photographs are used with permission.

Finding Edith

After Edith Watson's death at Christmas 1943, Victoria Hayward, Edith's partner of 32 years, closed Wild Acres, the family home and farm in Connecticut, and left for their cottage at Martha's Vineyard. There is no indication that Queenie—as girls named Victoria born during Queen Victoria's reign were often called—ever returned to Wild Acres.

By 1956 Queenie was in a nursing home and Wild Acres was in real trouble. For 13 years it had sat empty and deteriorating. Paint peeled. Windows broke. The outside staircase to the studio collapsed onto what was left of the lawn. Vines grew through the walls. Doors sagged, locks rusted. Obviously abandoned, it was an invitation to thieves and vandals. Neighbours watched as strangers took away one truckload after another of furniture, paintings by Edith and her sister Amelia, hand-painted photographs, china, glass, tools … anything they could transport and sell. Something had to be done.

Bob Watson, 40 years younger than Edith, was her first cousin. (At 80, Edith's long-widowed uncle Edmund had married the housekeeper. Bob was the youngest of their three children.) Bob and his wife, Lois, were Edith's closest relatives in terms of both blood and geography. In the summer of 1956 the couple obtained a court order to go into the crumbling house.

When Lois and Bob arrived at the house, they could only stop and stare. Lois had never liked Edith, whom she found abrupt and not at all interested in farming, husbands, or children. But she respected Edith and her work and believed in basic decency. This calculated theft horrified her. The disrespect it showed of people and their lives broke her heart.

The pair eventually picked their way toward the house through broken glass, dishes, and ornaments, bits of cutlery, and threadbare pieces of clothing. Frames from which Edith's and Amelia's paintings had been stripped lay scattered around the yard. Those watercolour and oil paintings still show up at auctions, having been who-knows-where in the interim. Dining room chairs waited on the porch for the next truck.

Inside, the first floor was empty, except for an old square piano, a high secretary-bookcase, and a Victrola. Family photographs remained

Edith at 30, about the time she started her travels to Canada. Photo by F. Warner.

on the walls among dark areas where paintings had been removed. Upstairs, the studio was empty (was this the work of vandals or had Queenie emptied it?), but the simple, painted bedroom furniture remained in Amelia's, Edith's, and Queenie's rooms.

The small trunk room at the back of the house was untouched, quite possibly because it was packed dauntingly full. Two bureaus and trunks with labels shouting Vancouver! St. John's! Montreal! Nassau! Quebec! competed for space with suitcases, clothes, size 3 shoes still caked with mud, tickets, souvenirs, postcards, books, cameras, a camp stove and pots and pans, notebooks, diaries, scrapbooks full of photographs and newspaper clippings, loose photographs, piles and baskets of glass-plate negatives, and Queenie's 10-inch-square portable typewriter in its wooden case. All these were wedged in every-which-way, falling over each other. That trunk room held the story of Edith's travels, on her own and with Queenie.

Lois and Bob's first inclination was to throw it all away. Even after looking through some of the scrapbooks, Bob was still convinced that they should let it all go. After all, the pictures weren't of family or even New England; almost all of them were from Canada and Newfoundland. But Lois had a different reaction. The more she saw, the more she knew that she couldn't let that happen. As she told me later, "There was something special there. I couldn't throw all that stuff out….Those two women loved that country so damned much."

Thousands of families of that era either threw away glass-plate negatives or scraped off the emulsion and used the glass to make greenhouses. The Watsons were no different and threw away bushel baskets of glass plates. Only 12 plates were kept, in a flat storage box stamped with *The Stanley Plate: Manufactured by Eastman Kodak Corporation, Rochester, New York*. Inside that box, on top of the negatives, Edith had left a handwritten note: "Heritage, Newfoundland."

Though they disposed of the vast majority of the plates, the Watsons kept every print they found. They stored the items they retrieved from Wild Acres in their second barn and spent evenings for two years going through it all, organizing it, and moving what they decided to save to two rooms and a large closet on the second floor of their house. Two weeks after they completed the work and had put the last of the materials away, the barn burned down.

The Watsons had a chicken farm to run (Lois hated chickens), five boys to raise (she loved every minute of it), as well as a community and an extended family to participate in. The boys married, moved, and had their own families. In 1979, at 65, Bob died. Through all that time and activity, Edith's things sat in those rooms, only occasionally looked at, but always cherished.

Then in 1982 a researcher from Canada wrote a letter asking about Edith and her work. Lois replied: "Who are you? What is your interest in cousin Edith?"

A photocopy of a photograph from a 1916 magazine had started my search for Edith S. Watson. It showed a woman at a loom with light pouring in a window. The woman was in the Magdalen Islands of Quebec, and the image was beautiful. It was also credited. One look and I was hooked. Who was the photographer? Where was she from? What other photographs had she taken?

I wrote hundreds of letters to archivists, magazines, curators, historians, librarians, photographers, photographic historians. I interviewed dozens of those people. My first assumption was that a photograph of a Canadian published in a Canadian magazine had been taken by a Canadian photographer. Canadian sources turned up more photographs by Edith, hundreds of them. Clearly this woman had been all over Canada, Newfoundland, and Labrador. She worked from time to time with a writer called Victoria Hayward. But no other information surfaced.

Speculating that the photographer could have been American, I repeated the query process in the US. Surely, somewhere, there must be a record of someone so prolific, the creator of such special and unusual work. Letters, diaries, articles, reviews. Anything?

The more I looked, the more images I found, the more these images—so many

Above: Chat at the bay, Crow Head [Queenie at right]. *Library and Archives Canada.* Over: On the pier head [Queenie at Gaspé].

of rural life, most often of women at work—fascinated me. I wanted more. I wanted the photographer's story. I began to hope that a book, or at least an article or two, might be possible. As my hope built, so did the dread of perhaps realizing that there was nothing to find.

After three years I had looked as far and as much as I could. Of all the letters I had sent out, only one, mailed more than a year earlier, remained unanswered, a testament to the dedication of librarians, archivists, and all the other people I'd contacted. I knew of nowhere else to look. I put together a pictorial article and was prepared to leave it at that.

Frances Rooney 11

Then a letter arrived from a woman who worked in a sub-basement of the Smithsonian. She had been so intrigued by my description of Edith that she'd looked way beyond the time frame I'd suggested (1914–28, based on the published photographs I'd found) and had found Edith in the 1955 edition of *Who Was Who*. The entry noted Edith's address as East Windsor Hill, Connecticut. A letter to the town clerk brought Bob Watson's name. Bob did not reply to my letter. Lois did.

Her letter changed everything. I hadn't mentioned my dream of publishing about Edith, but she offered: "There is a lot of material, enough, I think, for a book." I was thrilled. I was terrified. She agreed to meet to discuss the possibility of working with the materials.

In July 1982, I went to Connecticut and stayed at a motel on the outskirts of Hartford. It was there that Lois and I first met and looked each other over. We were both cautious, both reserved, both curious and intrigued. After half an hour of talking she invited me to start work the day after Labour Day. As I walked her to her car, she told me about the motel's less-than-wholesome reputation, of which I had been blissfully unaware, and said she'd wondered what kind of person she was on her way to meet. We parted laughing, looking forward to September.

For three and a half delicious months, from Labour Day until just before Christmas, Lois opened her house to me. She set me up with a table and chairs in the middle of Edith's and Amelia's papers, paintings, and photographs. She fed me, introduced me to people, and took me to Wild Acres and the cemetery down the road where Edith is buried. In her quiet way, Lois told me how she had loved having a baby pig or two in the kitchen when Bob was out and the boys were at school; she let me witness her grief over Bob's death and the courage and dignity with which she went on. She was a shrewd farmwoman who knew her worth and took pride in her life.

Once I'd been with her for six weeks and she'd had a chance to get to know me more, Lois took me to the attic space under the eaves—and two more trunks of letters, papers, and photographs. Another 5,000 pieces of paper, I estimated. I'd been busy, but now the pace became insane. I read and wrote and photocopied until I could no longer see, then went to the apartment I'd rented in Hartford or stayed at Lois's until the next morning, when it all started again.

I combed through letters, newspaper clippings, reviews of art shows and of *Romantic Canada* (the book Edith had done with Queenie), scrapbooks, maps, deeds, diaries, journals, account books, public records. I pored over photographs that were unlike anything I'd ever seen. They were beautiful. They were sympathetic to their subjects; their composition was stunning. They took me into worlds, into lives, a century back in time and from one coast of North America to the other.

Edith liked to photograph women. She made many sympathetic images of children and men, but the main body of her work portrays women. Perhaps she wished to redress the balance of representation of women and men in photographic records. Whether or not that is the case, she had an artistic fascination with rural settings and the women in those settings. She was drawn to women's energy and resourcefulness as well as the many facets of their lives. She found beauty in all kinds of women doing all kinds of activities.

Honest depictions of ordinary women are almost invisible in the perspectives of male photographers. When females do appear in late 19th- or early 20th-century photographs, they are often accessories to men or delicate creatures of decoration in a man's world. And women in photographs who are neither young nor pretty nor fashionably dressed are almost always someone's mother, obviously poor and defeated, or sex-trade workers.

Not in Edith Watson's work. She shows women and girls kneeling to draw water from wells, carrying loads of hay or spruce boughs wrapped in blankets and thrown over their shoulders, bending over fish on flakes. She records women carrying water in pails hanging from hoops in the remarkably simple practice that kept pails from hitting and injuring their legs, a practice only ever used in Newfoundland

Digging potatoes, Path End.

The women & children
harvest the hay, while
the men of the family
are away at the fishing.
Horses are unknown, in
many of these out-ports
of Newfoundland

In Fortune Harbour, where horses are unknown.

and Labrador. In her photographs, women cook in huge outdoor pots, bake in outdoor ovens, and scratch at the soil in rocky gardens. They care for their children. Under one photograph showing women carrying loads of hay into the top story of a barn she wrote, "In Fortune Harbour, where horses are unknown."

In Newfoundland and Labrador during the seasons Edith was there, since men tended to be away much of the time fishing or perhaps hunting or logging, women were more available to Edith's camera. Men were not front and centre, wanting their pictures taken. Although many men would have been happy to have their wives and children photographed, some would have demanded to appear in the photographs as well, and others would have prohibited women from having their pictures taken at all. If the preponderance of women subjects had occurred only in Newfoundland, it might be possible to speculate that Edith photographed so many women because men were away. But her focus was women wherever she went. And because it was, she has left a collection rich in the kinds of images seen nowhere else.

A note about how I refer to Edith. Many writers would use the full name of their "subject": Edith S. Watson, in this case, and less formally Edith Watson, or simply Watson. I use her first name much of the time. I do this with immense respect and affection. I do it to indicate a full human being with a rich and complex life in her family, work, and travels. I neither claim objectivity nor believe that it is possible, so I make no attempt to create a sense of objectivity or distance through form of address.

Many Victorian women of Edith's circumstances kept diaries or journals. Amelia Watson did. Queenie sometimes did. If Edith wrote diaries, they are long gone. But she did leave thousands of photographs. Many of the published ones can be identified, thanks to her insistence on credit lines (Edith *S.* Watson, not Edith Watson). And there are the Canadian and Newfoundland and Labrador albums, the record she precisely and lovingly compiled. Her legacy. Her story.

Somewhere out there are many more photographs that don't bear her name—those she gave away, left with friends and landladies; those whose origins have been lost in archives where lack of money, space, skill, or safe storage meant that photograph and photographer were separated.

Edith's photographs speak volumes. About Newfoundland, Labrador, and Canada. About the art and commerce of photography. About a woman who was a photojournalist before that term existed, and about her life, travels, and passion. Edith S. Watson wanted her work to speak for her and her life.

A daisy field in the Codroy Valley, at Little River

*By the Roadside
Hermitage*

"Edith Watson, Camera Artist"

In the summer of 1891 or 1892, a well-known, 30-year-old watercolour artist from Connecticut arrived on the ferry at Port aux Basques, boarded a smaller ferry, or perhaps a fishing boat, and headed off to explore Newfoundland and the fishing villages—known, she soon discovered, as outports—that clung to its coast. No one could have known that this would be the beginning of a lifelong love affair with the people, the way of life, the scenery, and the seemingly endless deep fjord-like inlets and bays of Newfoundland and Labrador. Nor could she or anyone else have guessed that within a few years photography would replace painting as her chosen art form; that she would spend almost four decades wandering this island colony, its mainland, and the new country to the west of it; that she would make her living as a travelling freelance photographer; or that she would leave thousands of remarkable images of the lives of people living in rural communities, most often women, at work.

The youngest of Sarah Bolles's and Reed Watson's four children, Edith Watson grew up on Wild Acres, a 16-acre tobacco farm on the Connecticut River in Reed's home village of East Windsor Hill, just outside Hartford. Compared to the Bolles family houses and the imposing brick structure in which Reed grew up (which Reed's brother, Edmund, a teacher and a harsh and unpleasant man, inherited), the clapboard house at Wild Acres was the runt of the litter.

Another of Reed's brothers, Sereno, earned an MD and a PhD in botany, and explored the western US and discovered several plants, which were named for him. He then settled at Harvard and worked with Asa Gray. Gray died after completing *Gray's Anatomy* but left *Gray's Botany* unfinished, and it was Sereno who completed the work. He also taught photography at Harvard, perhaps informally. He was gentle, kind, quiet to the point of shyness, and adored by his entire family. They loved his visits and wished he could spend more time at Wild Acres. It is probable that on one of his visits there he gave Edith her first camera and taught her how to use it.

Childhood at Wild Acres sounds like a kind of Victorian idyll. When Edith was born in 1861, Rosella, the oldest child, was eight, Donny six, and Amelia five. A hired boy helped on the farm and a young girl, Charlotte, worked in the house until Sarah realized, with huge regret, that Charlotte was helping herself to things that were not hers and had to be let go. When Rosella was little, she and Sarah enjoyed leaving letters for each other in the family mailbox by the road. Rosella was the intellectual gem of the family and her artistic talent appeared very early. Donny played with the animals in the yard, chased balls in summer, skated and sledded in winter, delighted in life on the farm, and found joy in his studies, including Greek and Latin. Like Rosella, Amelia's talent for painting became evident early, and by the time she was 18 she was teaching art.

Then along came Edith. Brainy, independent, stubborn, and impatient from the beginning, her kind of temperament proved disastrous for many Victorian girls. But the people around Edith enjoyed her spirit, and letters from her father emphasize his pride in her and his confidence that she would live a resourceful, successful, and prosperous life. Nowhere in the family papers is there any indication of pressure on the girls to marry.

The children briefly attended their Uncle Edmund's school. For the most part, though, Sarah taught them at home. The only sibling for whom there is any clear record of higher education is Edith. She graduated from Hartford Female Seminary,

at Little River.
In the Codroy Valley.
showing the home of
the Doucets, where
we boarded.
Mr. Doucet acted
as guide to the tourists

23

Two women, four buckets.

founded in 1823 by Catherine Beecher, sister of Harriet Beecher Stowe, who taught there on occasion. Some female seminaries were little more than finishing schools, but Beecher wanted Hartford Seminary to be a leader in opening the way for women's higher education in the United States. She set up a rigorous curriculum that included history, Latin, Greek, and mathematics as well as training in music, art, and the finer points of being a New England lady. For Edith, the school also built on the foundation she had gained at home of valuing friendship among women and relying on herself. Aside from having to learn Latin, she enjoyed Hartford Seminary. Her graduation program and a dance card from the graduation festivities, as well as notes and cartoon drawings about the horrors of studying Latin, remain in her papers.

No idyll can go on forever. In 1875, Donny died suddenly and mysteriously.* He was 20, Edith 14. Rosella worked with Sereno for several years and produced a series of luminous botanical drawings, which stayed in the botanical library at Harvard. In 1882, at 30, Rosa, too, died. The circumstances and location of her death remain unknown. At the time Amelia was teaching art at Temple Grove Seminary, in Saratoga Springs, New York. Edith had recently graduated from Hartford Seminary.

Soon after graduating, Edith hitched the family donkey, Jaffa, to her cart and went on a two-week wander around Connecticut and western Massachusetts. Jaffa held a high place in the family's affections. Edith photographed her with her cart, and Amelia painted a small watercolour of her. Jaffa was a perfect travelling companion. Together Edith and Jaffa made their way along the roads and inns to the Berkshire Hills, stopped for a short visit with Sarah's relatives, travelled eastward in Massachusetts, then worked their way home. At the end of the trip, Edith noted: "Cost of my trip, $5.00." This trip is significant: it marks the start of Edith's independent travels, it demonstrates her attention to money and costs (a lifelong obsession), and it indicates the family support she enjoyed. Support was not often available to Victorian women; independence had to be fought for.

---

* Several years after the publication of *Working Light* in 1996, Lois Watson sent me a newspaper clipping: "A Carefully Arranged Suicide." Donny had gone into Hartford, bought a small stove and a supply of coal, rented a room in a rooming house, sealed the room, and gassed himself. The owner of the house found him the next morning. Beside him were a small bottle of wine, untouched, a bag of orange peel, some maple sugar, a note saying "My name is Donald Watson. My parents reside at East Windsor Hill. My father's name is Reed Watson," and a letter addressed to his mother.

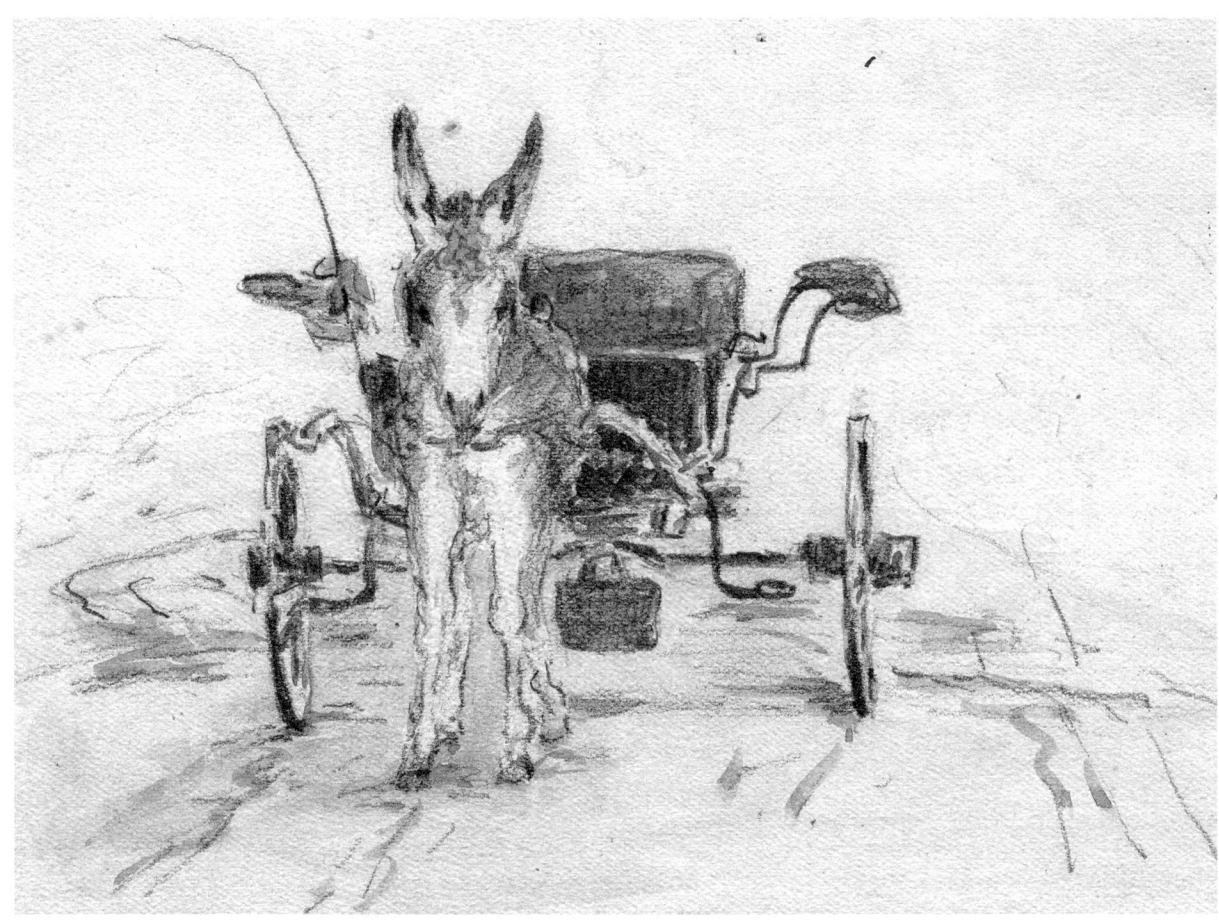

Jaffa, watercolour by Amelia Watson. Connecticut Digital Archive.

Amelia returned home for good the next spring. During her time in Saratoga Springs she had established a reputation as an artist and had held several successful shows. Edith joined her in shows and sales. For the next several years they painted at and around Wild Acres, and once winter had passed, took trains and buses around New England, going from one show of four or five days to the next. Edith administered and coordinated finances, schedules, and transportation for them and their paintings; Amelia dealt directly with the galleries.

Their schedules required stamina and brute strength. The two artists loaded packing boxes with paintings, took the boxes to the bus or train station, went to the city or town of their next show, picked up the boxes at the station, got them

"A Modern Evangeline"!
In Petty Harbor.
Nfld.

to the gallery, unpacked the paintings, hung the paintings, attended the opening, and were available for discussion with buyers or gallery owners for the duration of the show. They then packed the paintings back into the boxes, took them to the train or bus station, accompanied them to the next stop, and on it went. Since

shows routinely included more than 100 pieces, the sisters had to either carry enough paintings for an entire tour or arrange to bring in more stock from Wild Acres along the way.

Wherever they went, Edith and Amelia and their work were well received. Sales were good. The newspaper reviews that Edith collected in scrapbooks tended to note that the work of "Miss Edith Watson" was competent, pleasant, and attractive. Edith's talent certainly enabled her to make a living selling paintings.

But while Edith was, in a sense, marking time while she looked for her focus and purpose, Amelia was the greater talent and had developed a single-minded dedication to painting. Amelia's work shone. Amelia was the star of the show.

After the first year the sisters had a second-floor studio built onto the side of the house at Wild Acres. Precisely designed to meet the needs of two artists as a work and show space, two walls consisted

Left: The public well in Burgeo, has to serve the whole community.   Above: A breezy day, Burgeo.

Frances Rooney   29

almost entirely of glass, and an outside staircase provided access and privacy for both the studio and the rest of the house. The glass caused a stir in East Windsor Hill; the outside staircase created a sensation.

In 1887 Sarah bought a cottage across the road from the beach on Martha's Vineyard, an island nestled five miles by ferry between Cape Cod and Nantucket Island. One major attraction was Martha's Vineyard Summer Institute, an outdoor summer school whose students, most often women, included teachers, people who wanted to experiment with some art or craft, and highly proficient practitioners wanting to further develop their skills in the company of like-minded people. For two decades Amelia headed the art department and taught at Martha's Vineyard Summer Institute. Her reputation drew students, many of whom returned summer after summer. When Edith was not travelling, she spent at least part of every summer with her mother and sister in this place that would provide a retreat for the women of the family until 1956.

Two children.

During the fall and winter, Edith and Amelia continued to paint in their studio at Wild Acres and travel a circuit of galleries. The studio enabled them to add a kind of salon to life at home: friends came and stayed for several days or a few

An Eskimo home at the Moravian Mission, Hopedale, Labrador.

weeks, wrote or painted, and wandered the grounds at Wild Acres. From time to time other invited guests joined the groups for an afternoon or evening, and on occasion the studio was opened for public viewings. The sisters were able to work among and visit with their friends, meet new people, and sell their work directly from the studio.

Life was pleasant and prosperous. Many people in their position might have wanted to continue these rhythms and patterns indefinitely. Not these two.

In the early 1890s, reviews of Amelia's exhibitions noted that her paintings had started to include scenes not only from New England but also occasionally from

Nova Scotia and, more often, down the US coast as far as Florida.

As Amelia headed primarily south, Edith ventured north and east—once Edith stepped off that ferry in Port aux Basques, she was hooked. Even later, as her travels took her west into and across Canada, she would return to Newfoundland most summers for almost 40 years.

Why Newfoundland? Why not the warm weather, gentle and beautiful terrain, comfortable lodgings, and like-minded people of the Carolinas, Florida, or any of numerous other places? Newfoundlanders and many who have visited the province can see why she could fall in love with the place and keep going back. And back and back.

But why go to Newfoundland in the first place?

We may never know. Perhaps precisely because the US south was gentle, warm, beautiful, and familiar and had like-minded people. Maybe because she wanted to strike off alone, explore somewhere no one she knew was going, somewhere exotic and mysterious.

Whatever her reasons, two factors may have played a part in her decision: a general awareness of Newfoundland among New Englanders and access to travel between the two regions.

Virtually every literate New England family in comfortable circumstances subscribed to, passed among their friends and families, and devoured literary magazines. Travel was a favourite subject—writers regularly extolled the glories of Italy, France, England, the US west, and Canada. They wrote of Newfoundland both as startlingly beautiful and as a paradise for recreational hunters and fishers. While few of these people actually went to Newfoundland, they did keep a romanticized image of Canada and with it Newfoundland before their readers.

People who had migrated during the Irish potato famine in the 1840s, as well as people of French, Spanish, Basque, Portuguese, and English origin, had family connections in Newfoundland and New England. Fishers mingled on the Grand

Right: Bread and milk time for baby is puss's lunch time, too! In Shoe Cove.

Stocking a "fish
run", Shoe Cove

View of harbour with many masts.

Banks and up and down the coast. The constant stream of some young men and more young women going to (or home from) the "Boston States" to work ensured that coastal people from Hopedale to New York City were at the very least aware of each other.

Travel to Newfoundland was relatively available, comfortable, easy, and direct by late 19th-century standards. While a 2017 traveller might find it overly demanding to take a full day to get from Hartford to Port aux Basques or St. John's, to Edith three or four days constituted a fine journey made in good time. Mainland railroads ran frequently, including a Cape Breton line that ran to North Sydney starting in 1880. Several steamship and transport lines, among them Cunard and Red Cross, ran routes from St. John's or Port aux Basques to North Sydney or Halifax/Yarmouth, then on to ports in Maine, Boston, and New York. Ships

Spruce boughs for firewood, Hermitage.

to or from Europe stopped at St. John's and some or all of those US ports. Some ships also went on to Bermuda. The overnight ferry between Sydney and Port aux Basques made three round trips a week in summer and two, weather permitting, in the other seasons. Fishing boats regularly made part or all of the journey among those areas. In 1891 the fare from Boston to Halifax, via Annapolis, was $8.20. For under $20, Edith could get from home to Port aux Basques.

And there Edith was in 1891 or 1892, on the dock in Port aux Basques with her leather suitcase, carpet bag, and paints. She may have arranged lodging and transportation ahead of time. Or she may have stood there and wondered, *Now what?*

She may have taken just a few steps and boarded another ferry. Or maybe she spoke with the crew of a fishing boat who then took her to a home somewhere on the Burin peninsula where she could rent a room. During other trips she would stay a few nights here, a few nights there, with people recommended to her or with whom she'd boarded before. But during that first trip—and always—weather and the availability of transport determined when and where she painted and wandered, wandered and painted.

As Edith explored this intriguing and beautiful new land, photography gradually occupied more and more of her interest and attention. After the first few years, her luggage included a camera. Another year or two, and her paints stayed home. Her earliest extant Newfoundland photographs date from 1894, the same year one newspaper noted that "Miss Edith Watson, the well-known water color painter" had "brought her camera with her this season." By 1900, she was being referred to as "Miss Edith Watson, the camera artist."

She boarded with local families. She met people, made friends, and, as the photographs show, shared their trust and perhaps affection. They allowed her to see them in their ordinary activities and in their varying moods—happy, sad, angry, energetic, rebellious, tired. In many photographs it is clear that these people are enjoying having their picture taken. Together they and Edith created image after image of their lives. She had found her medium and her work.

And she had found her product. Photography was no leisure activity; she had a living to make, and as newspapers and magazines printed more and more photographs, she found a lively market opening to her.

Edith the business manager came into her own. She was already experienced in arranging travel, booking places to stay, and getting her work from place to place. Starting with her Newfoundland adventures, she paid with photographs for passes on railroads, local ferries, and the Cunard Line. The major photographic supply companies—Kodak, Ansco, Frontenac—exchanged materials for one-time use of prints in advertisements. Kodak and Ansco offered cash payment per print or double the cash value in paper and chemicals. These exchanges were crucial to

Above: In Bay St. Lawrence. Right: Heads and tails, Path End.

maintaining the constant travel and photographic supplies her work required.

Edith provided illustrations for travel brochures for the governments of Nova Scotia and Newfoundland. Large companies contracted with her for publicity photographs, including the CNR and the CPR, the Cunard Line, several rope and cartage companies, and Ginn educational publishers, as well as the Methodist Church. Newspapers from Halifax to Boston to Hartford to New York to Montreal to Toronto and as far west as Vancouver published her work. She sold prints to manufacturers of barrels and exporters of buckets. The *Canadian Magazine of Politics, Science, Art and Literature* published and credited almost 400 of her photographs between 1914 and 1925. Numerous other publications used her work, including *The Touchstone, Saturday Night, Travel, Yachting, Town and Country, Arts and Decoration, National Geographic, Asia, Ladies Home Journal*, and even such unlikely clients as *Vogue* and *Hygeia*, the journal of the American Medical Association. Some clients approached her either while she travelled or

No running water here! A public well serves the whole community in many Nfld. outports.

at home in Connecticut; others she contacted and sent sample prints to initiate sales. Through this informal system, her photographs of women carrying water on hoops, of children at community wells, and of women on the fish flakes made their way to cities across North America and sometimes to England and Bermuda. The better her work sold, the more she could do.

In 1900 Edith began to spend winters in Bermuda. The contrast between outport Newfoundland, where people worked long and hard in difficult, even brutal, conditions, and the Bermudian playground of the rich could hardly have been greater. As is the case with Edith's trips to Newfoundland, what prompted her first visit to this other island is unknown. It is probable that Cunard hired her to travel on one of their ships and supply them with photographs of its North American ports of call: St. John's, Boston, New York, and Bermuda. From then on, Bermuda became part of her annual pattern: late spring, summer, and early fall in Newfoundland and/or some part of Canada, Connecticut from the US Thanksgiving in late November to Christmas, and Bermuda from early in the new year until she returned to Wild Acres for Easter.

Bermuda was charming, luxurious, and gently warm. Had that been the extent of the island's appeal, she never would have gone back as often as she did. For a professional photographer, spending time in Bermuda was a shrewd business move. Edith lived and worked in a cheap rented studio among the year-round population and sold everything she could produce: photographs, paintings, and that immensely popular hybrid, hand-painted photographs. In Bermuda, as at Wild Acres, she sold out of a studio. Bermuda also offered another large and affluent market: the hotels fostered art, artists, and art (or souvenir) collectors by inviting a resident artist to settle into the hotel lobby each day for several weeks. The artist worked, chatted with the clientele, made useful contacts, and sold her work. Edith did this for 20 years.

By early in the new century Edith's summer wanderings were taking her to Quebec as well as Nova Scotia and Newfoundland. Ontario and Manitoba would soon be added to the list, and by 1920 she had worked her way across

Mending nets, Fortune Harbour.

Canada to the west coast. But while many locations in Canada certainly provided new opportunities for travel, work, and sales, she kept returning to Newfoundland.

At Wild Acres after 1900, Sarah and Reed were slowing down. Amelia stayed with them and painted and sold work from home. Edith travelled, sold photographs, and sent money home. Reed's letters to Edith in these last years of his life indicate that he was proud of his daughters and, at the same time, regretted that he had not been able to fulfill his early plans of accumulating wealth. It especially saddened him that the farm, bought in 1851, had been remortgaged more than once, and was still not paid for.

Reed died in 1905. He was 82. Edith was away completing a contract and could not get home. She was at Wild Acres when Sarah, three years younger than Reed, died just before Christmas 1910. After Sarah's death Edith made a postcard with a photograph of her mother on it in a classic Whistler's Mother pose. On the back of the postcard, Edith wrote, "Now we are just two from our little family of six." Edith was 49, Amelia 56.

Amelia went back to travelling, painting, teaching, exhibiting up and down the coast, and spending summers at Wild Acres and the Martha's Vineyard cottage. Edith travelled, sold photographs, and checked in at Wild Acres twice a year. It was a pleasant and productive routine. But while Edith's professional life continued and grew steadily, her personal life was about to change beyond recognition.

In spring 1911 friends introduced her to Victoria Hayward, a 35-year-old journalist and Bermuda native recently returned from teaching math in a boys' private school in New York state. Queenie was easygoing, smart, occasionally mischievous, and fun. She had a quick smile and a gentle sense of humour, loved being outside, and was eager to explore new places and meet new people. Physically she resembled Amelia: graceful, agile, and pretty. She took neither herself nor her work overly seriously and was at ease in social situations.

Edith spent that summer in Newfoundland, and visited Ellen Moore, her friend from Hartford Seminary, in Ste. Anne de Beaupré en route home to Wild Acres. In the fall, Amelia wrote in her diary, "Edith's Bermuda friend coming to visit." Queenie did visit, and the next spring, when Edith went to Bermuda, she and Queenie entered the life/work/travel relationship that lasted 32 years—the rest of Edith's life. Whether they got to Newfoundland that next summer is unclear, but a series of photographs documents their time in Labrador in September 1913.

Edith and Queenie, though temperamentally different, complemented each other extraordinarily well. Both loved islands and the sea. Edith's travel and work schedule would have exhausted most people. Queenie thrived on it. Edith could be impatient, sharp, and judgmental; ambition and financial necessity kept her

On board "the Stellarton." Mr. Willis studying the chart on way to the Goose Arm. Capt. Thos. Borland at the wheel.

always running. Queenie was gentle, accepting, and easily amused, especially with Edith. Edith was the administrator, Queenie the diplomat. Queenie eased the world's dealings with Edith and Edith's dealings with the world.

The pair occasionally collaborated on illustrated articles, particularly for the *Canadian Magazine*. Unfortunately, Queenie was inconsistent in her work and she paid little attention to deadlines. Letters indicate the growing impatience of magazine editors when Edith's photographs arrived in good time and Queenie's article arrived late or not at all. Sometimes the photographs were published on their own; sometimes editors cancelled the contract and returned the unpublished

On the fish flakes, Burgeo.

photographs to a very frustrated Edith.

Ambitious and practical, Edith did all the bookkeeping and conducted most of the business negotiations. Her need for artistic and commercial recognition meant that publishers and other potential clients had to see her name as well as her work. In an era when photographs were often considered throwaway space fillers whose creators did not merit mention, she insisted on, and received, good prices for her work *and* credits in print. Without the prices and credits, she could not have continued as a professional photographer. Without those credits, her work would have been irrevocably lost to the abyss of Anon.

When World War I began in August 1914, everyone thought it would be over

Above and left: In Path End.

by Christmas. No one dreamed that it would be a slaughter and a catastrophe. Men and boys enlisted in huge numbers. Ninety per cent of the soldiers who went over the top at Beaumont-Hamel were lost. That overwhelming loss, and further losses at Vimy and Passchendaele, affected every family in Newfoundland and the mainland. The women who were nurses at or near the front or in Britain worked in horrible and dangerous conditions, sometimes on 20-hour shifts and living on starvation rations of bread and sugar. Their exact numbers are not known.

Ships and boats were drawn into the war effort. Women struggled to keep households going and families fed with even fewer resources than usual. Some worked in munitions factories and stepped into traditional male jobs, and many others, including almost all outport women, rolled endless bandages and knitted, often from the wool they had sheared from their own sheep, hundreds of thousands of socks, mittens, scarves, and blankets. With all that was going on and the greater-than-usual demands on the people at home and overseas, travel to Newfoundland was both difficult and ill-advised. Not knowing how long it would be until they could return, Edith and Queenie went elsewhere during the war years.

Although it meant no Newfoundland trips, the war expanded work possibilities for Edith. She negotiated contracts that took her and Queenie to Cuba, Mexico, and Nassau, and their travels in Canada continued.

Edith and Queenie took advantage of the fact that many sailing ships had been brought out of retirement to carry fir and pine planks to Britain. Some of these vessels had figureheads. The elaborate and often beautifully carved figures of women used as figureheads on ships had long fascinated Edith and she had already accumulated photographs of them from Newfoundland to New York. Now she took more photographs of figureheads, notably in Boston Harbour and West Bay outside Parrsboro, Nova Scotia. Getting close to the figureheads was not difficult: hire a boy with a boat to row her around the harbour. Then, in full ladylike dress, twist and turn in the boat or climb in the rigging on the ship to get the right angle for a good shot. The images attest to the difficulty of getting them. Unfortunately, no photographs of Edith as contortionist have been found.

During the war, Edith corresponded with Peter Verigin, leader of the Doukhobors, refugees from Russia who had settled on government-granted land in parts of Saskatchewan, Alberta, and British Columbia. After two years of letters, Verigin invited Edith and Queenie to visit, and they spent much of the summers of 1917, 1918, and 1919 in Doukhobor communes, taking photographs and participating in the newcomers' way of life.

Peace brought a time of mixed blessings and curses. Many returned soldiers were shattered mentally, physically, or both. Then in 1919, Spanish flu ripped around the world, hitting Newfoundland hard and killing half the population of Labrador.

For self-supporting women, including Edith, it was a time of great difficulty. Men coming back from overseas took many jobs from women, including work

An Interior
Burin, Nfld

In Hopedale, Labrador.

that Edith could have expected to do. Peace brought continued expansion in publishing, and more and more newspapers and magazines published photographs, including several of Edith's Newfoundland images. But one after another, steamship companies, railroads, and photographic supply companies stopped using the barter system she had relied on and insisted on upfront cash payments. Finally, a glut of photographers meant that work, price per photograph, and Edith's income decreased.

Ever resourceful, she and Queenie launched off in a new direction. In 1920 Queenie noted in a small staple-bound booklet: "Our Book. I begin work on it. Nov. 12." Macmillan Canada published *Romantic Canada*, Edith and Queenie's most significant collaboration, at the end of 1921. At more than 250 pages, with 76 photographs, it was the largest and most lavish travel book to come out of

At the Moravian Mission, Hopedale, Labrador.

Canada to that time. Twenty-five-year-old Macmillan president Hugh Eayrs had taken over the debt-ridden, chaotic (thanks to the alcoholism of his predecessor) company just a few months earlier. He, Edith, and Queenie had high hopes for *Romantic Canada*, which was intended to be the new regime's headline publication and money-maker for the fall and Christmas season. But printers' strikes in Montreal and Winnipeg delayed its release by so many weeks that the first boxes of the book arrived at Macmillan on Christmas Eve. All evening Eayrs ran the gauntlet of torrential rain to deliver copies to bookstores. Valiant though his efforts were, it was too little too late. Reviews lavished praise on the book. Sales never reached anticipated levels.

Chapter VII, "Newfoundland," opens: "Having stepped aboard the Newfoundland mail-and-passenger boat at North Sydney, a little before ten p.m., the hour of sailing, one awakes next morning at Port aux Basques, in Newfoundland, hardly aware that one is out of Canada, until the courteous Customs Official with 'Newfoundland' written on his cap, comes to examine one's baggage." The chapter praises the land, its scenery, the rigours of fishing, raising crops and animals, making clothing of the wool from the sheep, the independent spirit of the people, and the distinctive characteristics of individual outports.

Chapter VIII takes the reader to Labrador. Here Queenie describes how numerous stories of the Labrador "accumulate into a magnetizing force, drawing you to explore that wonderful Northern shore of which these old-timers relate such wonderful tales." She describes her and Edith's first crossing: "The Invermore blew out her tubes somewhere down the coast, and had to put back to Saint John's, and we had to wait several days for her substitute, who finally arrived in Twillingate in the middle of the night, so that we went up the ladder over her side with the bags of mail at two o'clock in the morning, carrying with us a feeling that perhaps we ought not to be going, as two old fellows encountered on the pier the night before, had said, in the face of a rather threatening sky, that is was 'too late to go down on the Labrador.'" Clearly, they went anyway, and lived to tell the tale.

The publisher's foreword to *Romantic Canada* notes that "the author and artist have gone from Canadian coast to Canadian coast. They have thought it not unwise also to include matter descriptive of their travels in Labrador and Newfoundland." Most reviews of the book comment on the inclusion of this other dominion (as well as the French islands of St. Pierre and Miquelon); none seems to find it inappropriate. Edith and Queenie clearly couldn't bear to leave it out. Readers and reviewers at the time of its publication cheerfully welcomed the pieces about Newfoundland and Labrador.

Edith and Queenie's travel continued in the 1920s: Vancouver Island, Haida Gwaii, Ste. Anne de Beaupre, the Magdalen Islands, Nova Scotia; Bermuda; up and down the US east coast. Interspersed with these other excursions were trips to Newfoundland. Edith's latest extant photograph is dated Newfoundland, 1929.

Hoeing potatoes, Petty Harbour.

The expense, difficulty, and complexity of Edith's work continued to increase. The *Canadian Magazine* and Frontenac Photographic Supplies closed down. Other companies she had long dealt with expanded and operated in more formal and complex ways. Proposals with Macmillan for three more books—*Romantic Bermuda*, *The Islands of Canada*, and a book on figureheads—fell through, despite the efforts of Hugh Eayrs with Macmillan in New York and London. Queenie's completed manuscript and the signed contract for *Romantic Bermuda*, along with

Left: In Exploits, the Church of England and rectory in the distance, the Rev. Mr. Bull rector.
Above: In Exploits where I boarded.

notes and photographs for the figureheads and islands books, went into a trunk.

Edith and Queenie spent more time in Connecticut and at the cottage at the Vineyard. The Great Depression in the years after 1929 necessitated rejuvenated efforts to sell, mostly from Edith's huge accumulated collection of material. Edith and Amelia also had to sell treasured family belongings. They managed to hold on to Wild Acres and the Vineyard cottage, perhaps in part because neither place would have found a buyer.

On December 27, 1934, Amelia boarded a bus for Orlando, Florida, where she was to set up an exhibition to open in January. Three days later, on her way to the gallery, she collapsed and died on the street.

As the 1930s went on, life grew more relaxed for Edith and Queenie. Sales continued. The women visited and corresponded with their large personal and professional networks across North America and beyond. Edith had registered to vote as soon as she could in 1919, and was an enthusiastic Democrat for the rest

In the Lane
at Petrie's

of her life. She followed the heated debates of the "Is Photography Art?" controversy, but since she refused to publish photographs without payment, she missed out on Stieglitz's Photo Secession and having her work published in the major publication in the history of photography, *Camera Work*.

In 1937, Edith and Queenie went to Europe. From Paris they travelled through southern France and into Italy, then north through Switzerland and Germany, to Le Havre, where they boarded a ship for home. They collected notes, snapshots, menus, postcards, and maps. Edith marked her map of Paris with an X to indicate their hotel room overlooking the Seine. It was a perfect final major trip for two spirited, dynamic women who had spent their lives exploring.

During the 1930s, too, Edith assembled albums of her Canadian and Newfoundland and Labrador photographs. Whether she intended it or not—and she very well may have—these constitute her legacy. They showcase the art and travels that made her remarkable life possible and the remarkable person who made the travels and art possible.

On December 14, 1943, Edith and Queenie took a six-and-a-half-day bus trip from Wild Acres to St. Petersburg, Florida. Edith arrived exhausted and complaining of terrible indigestion. The indigestion turned out to be ulcers; surgery was the only known treatment. She woke from the operation, spoke to Queenie, and died. Queenie arrived back in Hartford by train with Edith's coffin on Christmas morning. Edith had wanted her gravestone to be the same as her parents' and Amelia's. Queenie made sure that happened, but with one addition: Edith's stone bears the inscription, "They seek a country."

Edith had lived and worked intensely, intrepidly. Her first trip was alone with Jaffa. Five or six years of travels around New England with Amelia followed. Then, for 20 years she again travelled on her own, before (to her surprise) spending 32 years living and wandering with Victoria Hayward. Where most other photographers recorded urban life, rural areas and the people in them attracted her. Along the way she explored, recorded, and compiled a treasure of rich and

In the lovely Harbour of Burgeo.

vivid, dignified, and respectful images of lives at the turn of the century, most often women at work. Many of the finest of these come from outport Newfoundland and coastal Labrador and provide a record like no other of life among people who considered themselves ordinary but who shine out of Edith's photographs as independent, resourceful, and exceptional.

Spruce boughs.
for fire wood.
Hermitage.

Partial list of locations of Edith S. Watson's photographs.

Edith's Newfoundland and Labrador

What must it have been like to step off the ferry in Port aux Basques for the first time? It was morning, probably in June 1891 or 1892. If the fishing season had not yet started, it was about to, and the shore would have been busy with last-minute preparations—mending nets, checking repairs and maintenance of boats, finalizing arrangements with crews. If the season *had* begun, boats were going out and coming in; men on shore were unloading their first or second catch of the day before heading home for their second breakfast; others were on the way back to the boats to go out again.

Did anyone notice the straight-backed woman from away with her colourful carpet bag, leather suitcase, and unusual, thin wooden box? Did anyone see her taking in her new and so very different surroundings? See her drinking in the reality of this world she had for so long read and heard about?

The coast was wilder, rockier, more jagged than the one Edith knew, the breaking waves larger and more dangerous than those she was used to. During the overnight crossing from North Sydney she may have had her first awe-inspiring view of icebergs. She was familiar with the activities of commercial fishing, of wresting a life from the sea. Here, in Port aux Basques, though, far more women participated in the heavy work than she'd seen elsewhere. Pairs of women, or a man and a woman,

Frances Rooney 61

Monday morning by the Brookside, Hermitage. My home here with Mrs. Jos. Mercer.

trudged back and forth with loads of fish on wide planks or in barrels hung between two sets of handles. From the boats to sheds or from the sheds to large platforms known as flakes they went, leaving fish in the sheds or placing them on those flakes.

Almost 30 years later, Victoria Hayward—Queenie—would write in *Romantic Canada*: "There is often no road from one village to another, entrance and exit always being accomplished over the sea; by boat or steamer….These Newfoundland villages, products of the Sea and its Harvest … are as variable as the sea's own moods. So, in cruising among the Newfoundland bays, every little headland turned reveals a different grouping, as well as different setting, of the tiny church, the little homes, the chief store; and a different arrangement of the wooden stages

Petries Point, where I boarded, Bay of Islands in Birchy Cove.

in wharf-like lines along the irregular waterfront." Edith was in her element.

That first night, and hundreds of nights following, Edith boarded with a local family. The outport communities where her hosts lived ranged in size from a handful of people to several hundred. As Edith explored, she would occasionally stop in a town whose main income came from trapping, sealing, mining, logging, or herring or salmon fishing. But almost half the colony's population was involved in the cod fishery, and she usually stayed with fishing families.

Most outport houses consisted of two rooms—a kitchen and a sleeping room. Many were poorly constructed from imperfect lumber and could not keep out the wind, rain, or snow.

A snug harbor.
Nippers Harbor.

As we meet on the road, Hermitage.

The kitchen was the heart of the home and the most public space in the community. It was where most domestic activity happened. This was also where neighbours, friends, and relatives crowded in for a visit, a meal, a discussion of some political or social development and to tell stories and spread the latest news of births, marriages, deaths, or church or educational developments. Here, too, women laid out the community's newly dead.

With anywhere from six to 20 children crowded into one or two beds, with overflow on the floor, privacy did not exist. A few affluent families, most often those of the local merchant, might live in solidly built two-story houses of four or more rooms, some of which boasted mansard roofs.

View of the bay with ships.

Between these two extremes were those couples or widows/widowers whose children had died or grown and gone and who welcomed the added income and perhaps the company of a boarder. Edith photographed a few of the people she boarded with. One of these was Mary Hannaford of Petty Harbour. Mary was a widow whose three daughters, aged one, three, and five, were buried beside their father in the old Catholic cemetery. Her 31-year-old son had also died. This is the kind of house where Edith would have stayed most of the time.

The timing and duration of Edith's Newfoundland and Labrador trips varied from year to year, but she was generally in the region sometime between late May and mid-November. Depending on how far north or south she was, and whether she was on the island or the Labrador mainland, she could have been there before,

Dismantling the great whale, Snooks Arm. A work that always fetches an audience if carried out ashore!

during, and/or after the fishing season. Thus, while she was usually in the communities to witness the catch, cure, and sale of fish, the variety in Edith's locations and accommodations ensured that she witnessed a range of outport domestic, economic, religious, political, community, and work life as they played out through the rhythms of three of the four seasons.

Although Edith did not experience outport winters, she most certainly heard about them and saw the results of that season's work. Winter was a time of relative ease for the men. Not so the women. While the number of outside jobs for women decreased, the difficulty, even danger, of those jobs increased. The most important daily chore was getting water. Women collected water every day but Sunday all year, whatever the weather. The community well could be several miles

Drying the Trap
Seines in
Nippers Harbor,
Nfld.

away, and the walk had to be made at least once a day, double that on Saturday to be ready for Sunday, and more than double again on Monday, wash day. A long walk over uneven, rocky ground in summer grew treacherous in winter snow, ice, and wind, particularly given that many women's shoes provided little protection from the cold, and clothing was not always adequate to protect them from weather conditions. Once at the well, ice had to be broken and the water drawn. The women then made their way home again, carrying water buckets hanging from hoops that protected their legs.

Capt. Borland on board "The Stellata" off Penguin Head, bound for the Goose Arm, Sep. 8, 1902.

Animals kept through the winter had to be fed and watered twice a day, and, if at all possible, protected from the worst of the cold. Women could collect milk in their aprons, where it froze as it came from the cow. Livestock were butchered as needed for food, perhaps a pig or a cow at Christmas.

Inside the house, warmth existed only around the stove, assuming that the wood supply lasted until spring. Water in buckets froze overnight. Laundry hung on the outside line froze, so that taking it into the house meant negotiating sheets of ice in the snow, cold, and wind. In winter women and girls cleaned the wool they had sheared during the year from the sheep. Once clean, the wool was carded, spun, and, for special garments, dyed. Knitting went on all winter: petticoats

Dogs with clogs. A cod protection, Shoe Cove.

and blankets as well as mittens, sweaters, socks, underwear, and shirts for the entire family. Wool ends were braided into rugs.

Relatively well-off people might buy other clothing at local stores, in St. John's at Ayre's, or off a boat that came round from Boston in good weather. But in many families, the mother and older girls made everything from underwear to coats, wedding dresses, army uniforms, and sometimes men's dress suits. A few people could afford to buy material by the yard. Many women, though, made clothes from flour sacks turned inside out and perhaps coloured with plant dyes. When worn spots appeared on clothing, the women turned cuffs and collars, shortened hems, patched knees. Hats too dirty to wear were turned inside out, concealing the dirt next to the wearer's head.

The winter following good growing and fishing seasons meant enough to eat: vegetables from the garden stored in a root cellar outside the house; preserved berries; lamb, pork, beef, or chicken (especially at Christmas) for those who had livestock; and of course fish, entire cod for those who could afford it, cheeks and stomachs for those who could not. People who could afford to used these less appetizing cod parts for fertilizer; needing to eat them meant poorer soil, further depleting families' nourishment and chances of survival. For everyone a poor summer, the death of a parent, or a particularly long and harsh winter often meant hunger, weakness, and illnesses—even starvation and death—brought on by poor nourishment.

By the time Edith arrived in spring, the full load of outside work was well under way. Keeping up with the rhythm of outport life could mean the difference between making it through the next winter and not. Even though the coastal soil was thin, poor, and rocky, many fishers also farmed. Men cleared the land. Some also prepared it for planting. The women took over from there with help from the girls and sometimes young boys. They planted, weeded, fertilized with fish heads and stomachs, and tended vegetables, mostly potatoes, turnips, carrots, and onions. When the crops were ready, the women harvested them, prepared some to

At the Spring.
Nippers Har.
Nfld.

eat or sell, then put the rest aside for the winter by canning or making fruit preserves.

Men may have let the livestock out in the morning. Sheep, goats, pigs, chickens, and geese stayed close, either in pens or free in the yard. Cows wandered, often great distances. At dinnertime the women searched until they found the cows, then led them home and milked them.

Getting in wood for the winter began again in early spring. Generally, men chopped the largest pieces, leaving them where they had been cut. Women collected the wood, took it home, cut it to a useable size, and stacked it. They also collected spruce boughs. Firewood was only the beginning of the uses of the incredibly versatile spruce. It was also used to make spruce beer, a rising agent for bread, and protective coverings for drying fish. Tender shoots were fed to cattle.

As all this and more was going on, everyone was gearing up for the fishing season: trappers and line fishers, those who went alone or with their families to the Labrador for the entire season, those who went to the Grand Banks, and those—the vast majority—who were inshore fishers. The men prepared boats, nets, and equipment for the gruelling schedule of trips out and back, out and back, day after day, week after week.

The dangers of the sea are well and vividly documented. The perils of being a woman living in outport Newfoundland have received almost no attention. Women were overworked, often undernourished, and weakened by constant pregnancy and nursing as well as miscarriages or abortions, and stillbirths. Until well into the 20th century, the largest single killer of women was complications of childbirth. A man lost at sea is a hero. A woman dead beside her newborn infant is invisible, as are the girls left to raise their siblings at the death of their mother.

The fishing season was longer in the south of Newfoundland, shorter along the northern coast of the island and Labrador, but from June to October, and especially in July and August, hard lives, many of them lived on the knife edge of subsistence, turned into a blur of activity. Men fished, tended the boats, ate, and slept.

As you meet them on the road!

Women and girls as young as three did the rest. The youngest ones fed chickens, watched even younger children, and even stirred the lard and lye mixture on the stove to make soap.

Women's work, already complex, physically demanding, and essential to both the creation and the maintenance of life, grew even more complex and difficult during the fishing season. Three meals a day became seven for the men of the house, and added crew members meant even more mouths to feed: a "first breakfast" before the men went out, then a full dinner after each run, and a final meal at night before fishers and crews fell into bed. Women grew, harvested, fed, butchered, cured, and tended whatever was eaten. They made additional trips to the well for water. They organized, baked, roasted, fried, boiled, set up before a meal, served, cleaned up after every meal, and got ready for the next. Most women made bread every day or two, except during the fishing season, when they baked bread two or even three times a day.

Women did much of the work of "making" the fish. Men delivered the catch ashore. Both women and men cleaned and split the fish, drained excess water, and put them into vats of sea water. After five days, women or men washed the fish again with sea water and pressed the fish before taking them, often some distance, to the flakes. To carry the fish, two people held handles attached to opposite sides of either a rectangular piece of wood or a barrel. Each carrier could hold two quintals—224 pounds (100 kilograms).

This is where the women took over care of the catch. Each morning the weather allowed, they spread the fish on the flakes in the sun. At evening, they gathered them into faggots—round, waist-high piles more than one metre in diameter of skin-side-up fish topped by larger fish to protect the entire pile. The drier and smaller the fish, the larger the faggot, until the fish were dry enough and the piles were large enough to store for family use or to gather into quintals and sell for shipping to market. If all went well, the drying process took two weeks. While Edith was going to Newfoundland, prices for a 112-pound (50-kilogram) quintal varied from 3 to 10 cents, a meagre sum that rarely allowed a fishing family to cover its debts, let alone pay for the labour involved.

During drying, flies constantly threatened the catch and with it the family and community food supply and income. Women spent hours waving the flies away to keep them from laying eggs that would turn to maggots and ruin the fish. If eggs were laid, they had to be scrubbed off.

Women monitored the sky and air at all times. Given her experience on a tobacco farm, Edith was certainly familiar with the dangers to a tender crop and the urgency of protecting it. The fish had to be kept dry. Rain could wash out salt and leave the fish vulnerable to bacterial growth. High humidity could lead

to decomposition. Too much heat or sun, and the catch would scorch. A threat of rain meant dropping everything either to cover the fish with dried tree bark held down by boughs and rocks or to take them inside the stages along the shore. After a rain the women spread out the fish again on the flakes.

If fish were plentiful, they kept coming in, boat load after boat load. The new fish needed heading, gutting, splitting, salting, and spreading as the process continued and began again and again.

Above and left: In Hermitage.

The fishing season added hours of work to women's already 16- or 18-hour day. At peak times, they barely slept. Work on the flakes started by 6 a.m. While one or two women took fish to the flakes, others washed and spread them, then turned them as needed. On the ground beside the flakes young children took care of younger ones. Mothers sometimes carried very young infants with them or had them in a cradle beside them on the flakes. When a child fussed, the mother might tie a rope to her ankle and to the cradle and rock the cradle as she bent over the fish.

During the busiest weeks women worked until 2 or 3 a.m. They would then go home, fall into bed, and sleep until 5 a.m. or shortly after, when it was time to get the first breakfast for the men, who had been sleeping since right after their dinner the night before. On occasion a woman would stay all night on the flakes, either sleeping for a few minutes at a time, sometimes standing up, or not sleeping at all. It was a punishing schedule dangerous to healthy women, let alone someone who was pregnant and/or nursing or ill.

In all this tense activity, most people were too busy to notice a paying guest from away. For a photographer this was ideal: staying out of the way, she could wander and notice people and what they were doing, and then, when the time was right, provide a bit of fun by photographing them at their work.

Before, during, and after the fishing season, and given the amount of time she spent in Newfoundland, Edith experienced ordinary outport life as it went along. She must have seen weddings and funerals; the newly dead laid out in their houses; women caring for ill or injured people. She would have known women who were pregnant, nursing, or both without relief for 20 or more years after they married, sometimes pregnant at the same time their older daughters were. While she was there babies came into the world with the help of local midwives and babies died—almost a third of all deaths during that era in Newfoundland were among children under the age of five. It was well known that not all these deaths were natural. Records are sketchy, but they do show that an unusual number of young children died of "convulsions." Causes of those convulsions are not specified. She saw families decimated by diphtheria, tuberculosis, the ravages of malnutrition, and sometimes domestic or other forms of violence. The largest killer in North America at the time, tuberculosis, raged through Newfoundland as it did nowhere else (one woman in St. John's lost her husband and 11 children in one month, two children on the same day).

Edith met many young women and some young men who went off to the Boston states, to areas not far from her own home in Connecticut, where they worked as servants, labourers, or shop clerks before either settling there or returning home. Given the number of her trips and that she made return visits to many outports, she would have seen wives become widows, mothers who lost a child or women

In the Codroy Valley
On the road to
Tompkins.

Mr. W.E. Mills expert mining engineer.

who miscarried, became sterile, or died because of a botched abortion, young girls who disappeared for several months and lived in shame ever after, or whose aging parents suddenly and unexpectedly had yet another child.

The economic disparity in the outports, impossible to miss at any time, only became more obvious as many people did the work of catching and making the fish, while the privileged few did not. With rare exceptions, people in Newfoundland were either prosperous or struggling. Those who were not affluent grew and raised whatever they could and used materials at hand with impressive skill and resourcefulness.

But some things had to be bought, and this is where the eternal debt of many families originated. Without salt, for example, there would be no salt cod; without

Fish stages, St. John's.

salt cod, no survival. Salt, and some other supplies and equipment, could only be purchased. The agents who bought fish for use in St. John's or for export were the same people who sold the necessary fishing supplies. The price of those supplies was always greater than the selling price of the fish. It wasn't exactly "St. Peter don't you call me 'cause I can't go / I owe my soul to the company store," but it might as well have been. The result was the same. Somehow, even under this burden the fierce spirit of independence and individuality of the fishing families survived.

Poverty was not the only pressure on women. Social structure and its ally, religion, combined to define women's lives and to undercut their personal and public power. In the 21st century this might be termed "social control"; for the

Left: *Woman with bundle of hay, Fortune Bay.*   Above: Drying the great seines, Shoe Cove.

people in the outports when Edith was there, it was just Life.

Edith grew up in a place of religious variety and acceptance. Her immediate family were Episcopalians who, whatever the official stand of the church, lived with a kind God and a version of religion that supported their ambitions and their way of life.

The majority of people in Newfoundland outports were Catholic, with areas of Methodists and Anglicans, although most Anglicans lived in St. John's, and a few Congregationalists, Presbyterians, and Salvation Army members. In some places church attendance was mandatory, even if the church was a very long walk or a boat ride away. In other areas, services occurred when a minister arrived

In Nippers Harbour, in the "foy Free Zone" [a *foy* is a small boat used primarily to manoeuvre larger boats].

every three or four weeks. And in the smallest coves, neighbours gathered outside on a Sunday morning to sing a few hymns. But religion went far beyond Sunday morning.

Catholicism, particularly, emphasized that a woman's place was in the home, caring for her family and being subservient to her husband. In the outports, this put a woman in an ever-tightening vise of guilt: her religion told her to stay home and wait on people, the Victorian Angel in the House. If she did that, her family might very well starve. Her labour at home was crucial. So were her public functions: working on the flakes, tending the garden, rounding up livestock, fetching water, selling any possible fruits and vegetables as well as clothing she may have made for sale, perhaps taking in a boarder like Edith, serving as the community

In Nippers Harbour the home where I boarded above the cross in this little cove with Mrs. Joseph Batstone and Lovey.

midwife, caring for the sick, and dealing with the local merchants.

In 1890s Newfoundland slightly over half of school-aged children were in school. Schools ran according to religious affiliation, which meant that children of a religion other than the dominant one either could not go to school—even though there was one in the area—or had to go to other outports for school. In some places teachers spent a few months in one outport before moving on to the next or arrived for a few weeks two or three times a year. And in fishing time, as it is during planting time on farms, there was no school for anyone. When children were not in school, mothers, themselves with little or no formal education, taught them as best they could. It is to the women's credit that, despite the difficulties, more than half the people in the outports could read and/or write.

Late 19th- and early 20th-century Newfoundland, no surprise, was a male-dominated world. Female children started working early. Tasks that required brute strength were boys' work. The rest fell to girls and their mothers. Girls rarely made it to the age of five before they were performing regular duties in the house and garden or yard. They worked, boys often watched.

Then as now (there and elsewhere), marriages ranged from master-slave relationship to a partnership of equals at home. Although women needed to function in the outside world, the public realm belonged to men to the extent that women were barely visible. What they thought and felt almost never mattered. Women coped with the hand they had been dealt the best they could and in the ways women through time have always coped. Some enjoyed their roles. Some accepted and lived within them. Some found solace in religion. Some became miserable and bitter, manipulative, abusive, and violent. Some became politically active. Some turned into automatons. In "A Charm against the Pain," her poem from one Newfoundland woman to another, Geraldine Chafe Rubia put it this way: "She has a raging sorrow / She has unwitting grace."

Seventeen was considered a good age for a woman to marry. (This appears to be the low end of the spectrum; many women did not marry until well into their 20s.) Tradition dictated that fertility was the wife's responsibility; too few children or too many were her fault. That same tradition held that any visible defect, birthmark, or disability in a child came about because of something the mother had done or not done during pregnancy. Some men were gone 10 months a year, staying home long enough to start another child and then leaving the woman to get on with running the house, caring for the garden and livestock, and bringing up the children.

Unwed mothers were in some places tolerated, in others ostracized for their entire lives.

Adventurers from outside, like Edith, appear to have enjoyed a status outside the rules. Generally, single women were looked down on. Widows who could

Homeward bound.
With day camp and
spruce boughs.
Nfld.

In Hopedale, Labrador.

support themselves were perhaps best off: they might own property, they had a freedom other women could only dream of, and some owned and operated fishing vessels.

Much judging of women and their work went on as an undercurrent largely, as in other societies of people with little or no power, among other women. Nonetheless, it made for more work than may have been necessary. To be considered a good housewife, a woman had to keep a spotless house. That included washing the stove every day and scrubbing the floors with sand once a week. Laundry on the line deemed not clean enough was criticized.

At the end of the fishing season, once the boats and gear had been dealt with and some portion of the debt to the merchants paid, the men relaxed. This was their time for stories, for drinking with each other, for sitting with a pipe, for recovering from the weeks and months of fishing.

In White Bear, Labrador.

Women got no break. Winter was coming. The chores and rhythms of life went relentlessly on. In the autumn, if a child or children went to school, the mother had to fill the gap in work left by their time away. It was time to dig out any crops they had not yet harvested; to pick, can, and preserve berries; to gather and stack as much wood as possible for the winter; and to repair or if possible replace worn-out clothing and bedding.

Remembering that *Romantic Canada* was intended for the potential visitor, Queenie describes the joys of this season: "The surface of Newfoundland, its rocks and hills, is at its best in the fall of the year when the brush of Autumn pints all the foliage and fruit of the Bake-Apple, Partridge-Berries, wild red and black currants, Rowan berries, etc., gorgeous yellows, reds and browns. After the frost, the 'marshes and barrens' afford miles of colour."

She mentions gentians and orchids growing wild, and picking berries. "The best blueberries of all grow in the cracks and scarpings of the cliffs where one

would not suppose a thimbleful of earth could cling." And "What is more romantic than tea with the lighthouse-keeper's little family at Twillingate, where one sits at a spotless table and is served with a heaping dish of delectable homemade Partridge-berry jam smothered in thick Island cream?"

In summer, the population of Labrador doubled as fishing crews and often entire families virtually invaded the land of the Inuit and Métis. Edith probably went there in the 20 years she was going to Newfoundland before she met Queenie in 1911. An album of photographs taken in Labrador and clearly dated September 1913 includes five pictures of Queenie as well as shots—an iceberg, railroad lines and cars—quite unlike those in the personal album Edith left at Wild Acres.

Queenie wrote in *Romantic Canada* of her fascination with the people: the Métis, the Syrian fur dealers, the fishers and sealers, the Moravian Mission. Inuit carvings, their sealskin clothing, the tobacco pouches and wallets they sold to the arrivals by ship, and their dogs particularly intrigued her. She also ponders "the charm of the Labrador." As she wrote, "Some say … that it … lies in the fact that the slightest miscalculation on the part of those adventuring in these parts may lead to an accident—an accident that on so exposed a coast is instantly metamorphosed into irremediable disaster, as in the case of H.M.S. *Raleigh*. In other words, danger is its charm, the danger that lies so near, around the corner of every bay and tickle; danger of hidden rocks, of sudden gale, of fog, of bergs, washed by some fanciful twist of ocean current out of the beaten track." What a visitor found romantic or offered to distant readers in the comfort of their homes was a large part of what made this land so daunting for the people who spent part or all their lives there.

Album photographs give no indication of whether Edith knew the iconic medical missionary and author Dr. Wilfred Grenfell, and for a long time it looked as if that would remain an open question. Then, a small envelope fell out of a

Left: In Nippers Harbour.

On the highway, Petty Harbour.

In Venison Tickle, Labrador.

box of loose photographs, and in the envelope was a picture showing two women talking with a tanned white-haired man in a garden with palm trees—far from Labrador. A note on the back of the photograph says, "Edith, Queenie and Dr. Grenfell, Miami, Fla., on his birthday." Question answered.

Although Edith spent most of her time in Newfoundland and Labrador along the coastline and in outports, she did spend some time in St. John's. While almost no specific information is available, some reasonable speculation is possible. She would have met people who lived quite differently from those in the outports. She must have met or at least known of Elsie Holloway, Newfoundland's first woman professional photographer and finest 20th-century photographer. As a child Elsie occasionally went with her father, Robert, as he photographed outports in summers. After Holloway's death, Elsie and her mother and brother Bert published *Through Newfoundland with the Camera*, the compilation of many of his photographs. She studied portrait photography in England and, in 1908, opened a photography studio with Bert. He left to join the army in 1913 and was killed in

Off to the Banks, Nippers Harbour.

1916. Elsie ran the studio until she retired in 1946. Elsie was known for the quality and huge volume of her work, her skill and innovation in studio photography, and her images of landscapes. Somewhere along the way, in outports, in St. John's, or in both, Elsie and Edith had to have become aware of each other. They may very well have met.

St. John's was a place to replenish the photographic supplies Edith needed more quickly than they could come directly from Kodak or Frontenac. Tooton's Parisian Photographic Studio, usually known as Tooton's, opened in 1905 and had a major line of Kodak materials. Ayre's also sold photographic supplies as well as clothing and other necessities.

Edith was well aware of the importance of the vote and of labour unions for

2. Partridge Is.

In St. John's Harbour.

her and people like her. Before ever getting to St. John's, the centre of agitation for enfranchisement, she would have been party to outport women's discussions of getting the vote. The struggle in the US would gain her the vote in 1919; Newfoundland women would succeed six years later. And although she had some ambivalence about unions, the progress of unions and working women in them as a means to fair wages and safe working conditions interested her deeply, particularly after the notorious 1911 Triangle Factory Fire in New York City. It seems probable that in St. John's she would have met some of the people involved in these struggles.

In numerous visits over almost 40 years Edith Watson witnessed outport life as closely as anyone from away could. And she recorded what she experienced. The

The long shore road in Hermitage.

photographs she made stayed in drawers, on mantels, on dressers, and in family albums across Newfoundland and Labrador, and they went into the world in her and Queenie's book, in newspapers, magazines, and advertisements in Canada, the US, Bermuda, and England. And eventually she put her favourites into her personal album. Those unique photographs reflect her deep love of Newfoundland and its people, of a time and way of life that, like the island itself, were both terrible and beautiful.

• • •

A pesky mystery around Edith and the St. John's area remains. When I was researching *Working Light*, a friend looked at one of the prints I'd had made and said, "I've seen this before." That hardly seemed possible, given that these photographs had been out of view at least since the late 1930s, but she insisted.

Shortly after *Working Light* appeared, a woman in St. John's phoned. She was going to be attending a conference in Toronto. She had a large set of prints, some

Frances Rooney 97

Spreading Codfish.
Burgeo.

In Fortune Harbour and Mr. & Mrs. Cook, with whom I stayed.

of which she recognized from the book. She had taken snapshots of several of them. Would I like to meet, see her shots, and hear the story?

We met on a gorgeous June day outside Victoria College at the University of Toronto. Sure enough, while some of the images were familiar and others were not, these were all clearly Edith's work. I cannot to save my life find the woman's name, or she would get full credit here. She told the story she had heard of these pictures.

Several years earlier workmen demolishing a house in Quidi Vidi had found a tin box inside a wall. In the box were several very old negatives. The men looked at them, and like Lois Watson in Connecticut, decided that they should not be thrown away. They took them to a small gallery on Water Street. She did not

Women and children raking hay.

know the owner's name. This man accepted the negatives and made 500 sets of ten very large prints. The sets quickly sold out.

    The gallery owner, meanwhile, had done some undefined thing to displease a group of fairly rough people. Soon after selling the prints, he closed the gallery and went to work on an offshore oil rig. A few months later he disappeared from the rig, never to be seen or heard from again. Where the negatives went, who if anyone had them, nobody knew. Nor did anyone know who the photographer was, let alone how and why the negatives ended up sealed in a wall in a house. According to rumour, though, the photographer had been a familiar figure on the coast of Newfoundland and Labrador, where he spent many summers before going home to New England to spend the winter with his lady love.

The next fall a call came from a man in St. John's. He had seen *Working Light* in a grocery store, bought it, and loved Edith's work. He had also seen a set of large prints made from some negatives found in an old house in Quidi Vidi. Did I know them?

Um, … yes … and … ur … no. I told him about the woman I'd met.

The part of the story about the man who wandered the coast taking pictures had some truth to it: the man, however, was a woman; that woman was Edith. She did go back to New England for the winters, and who knew whether there was or was not any love interest. Yes, broadcaster and filmmaker David Quinton said, that part of the story was true, and yes, there was some mystery here.

Mr. and Mrs. Joseph Cook.

David and I corresponded for several years. We both wanted to make a film about Edith, and he was searching for money in Newfoundland and Nova Scotia, while I did what I could in Toronto. No film, but his efforts did result in a talk about Edith in St. John's. David met us at the airport, navigated the fog in his car while we followed in the rental. Once at the hotel, we had coffee and began a marathon conversation about just about everything. On day three, in a little café in the back corner of Bidgood's supermarket, we had soup and sandwiches under … a framed set of the photographs made from the negatives found in the wall in Quidi Vidi.

After lunch David introduced me to Linda Bidgood, who provided more

On the gallery, Path End.

pieces of the story. Her mother had owned a house in Quidi Vidi. In about 1970 she had the house dismantled and, yes, the workers found negatives in a cigar box in a wall. They were numbered and dated, 28 in all, from several places, including Bay of Islands, Placentia, Hermitage, Fortune, and Petty Harbour. The man in the gallery was Ron Mason and, yes, he did drop from sight.

From there it was surprisingly easy. Within days I had a long chat with Moya, one of Ron Mason's four children. Yes, he had owned Gallery Mason on Water Street. Those workers took the negatives from the wall to him at the gallery.

When he closed the gallery, quite possibly for financial reasons, Ron did go to work on oil rigs off the coast. He did not disappear, though; he worked on other oil rigs, some off Africa, was a baker, then chef, chief steward, and camp boss before returning to Ontario, where he designed and landscaped gardens in Toronto. He died in 2005 at 76.

Many questions answered, and several remain. How did the negatives get into that wall? Why? They show outport scenes—bays, flakes, boats, people, hardly the stuff of secrecy. Who lived in the house at the time? Did Edith stay in Quidi Vidi when she was working or making contacts in St. John's? Was it as simple as that she visited there and left the negatives behind? And finally, where are they now?

Over: Fishermen's luck.

Photography and the Photographs

Edith Watson became enthralled with photography exactly when photography had evolved to the point where she could both practice her art and make a living at it.

Modern photography began in 1839 with the nearly simultaneous revelations of inventions by Louis Jacques Mandé Daguerre in France and William Henry Fox Talbot in England.* While both processes had advantages, each also had shortcomings.

Daguerre's method produced sharp images. But those images, with their reflective silver sheen over copper, were difficult to look at, and each was one of a kind. Fox Talbot's approach led to diffuse images, but his invention of calotype paper meant that prints could be produced in multiples. And while Daguerre offered his invention freely to the world, Fox Talbot insisted on patent protection, which until the 1850s made his techniques almost inaccessible.

---

* Though numerous letters note her part in the development of her husband's process, including the addition of iodine to enhance paper's light sensitivity, little mention of Constance Fox Talbot is made in publications about her husband's work. If she is mentioned, it is usually to say that she was tremendously excited about her husband's work, that she was probably the first woman to take a photograph, and/or that she is buried with him and their children.

Fish stages, Petty Harbour.

Both processes were complicated: slow, expensive, and requiring much big, heavy, awkward equipment. Exposure times were long, often requiring the subject to remain absolutely still for four to six seconds or even longer. This combination rendered photography away from a processing lab and studio prohibitive.

Almost immediately, other inventors went to work to make photography faster, simpler, and cheaper. The mid-century arrival of wet plate collodion negative printed on albumenized papers made sharp images possible. But each negative had to be processed wet as soon as it was made, still requiring masses of equipment, including chemicals and a darkroom. Exposure times were still long. For all of that, these improvements did constitute major steps along the way to the kind of outdoor, quick, casual, way-of-life photography Edith Watson would want to create.

By the late 1870s, wet plate gave way to gelatin dry plate negatives. Photographic supply companies manufactured these plates, which could be stored, carried wherever the photographer wished to go, used as needed, and printed at any time. An easily created negative could be assembled ahead of time. The portable darkroom became obsolete and the improved sensitivity of the negatives shortened exposure time to the point where it was possible to photograph moving people or other subjects.

As all this had been going on, cameras had grown smaller and were about to take another leap in size. George Eastman's introduction of the first small, convenient Kodak camera in 1888 gave birth to the snapshot. The camera took 100 shots and was then mailed to the company in Rochester, New York, for processing. The photographer never opened the camera, never touched the film.

But Edith needed to do more than just take photographs. She had to sell them. And that required economical printing techniques for newspapers and magazines. The *Canadian Journal* began printing engraved images in 1853. Having to use engravings involved a long, complicated process very few magazines could afford. Those that used them did so sparingly.

In 1869 *Canadian Illustrated News* was the first publication in the world to print halftone reproductions on electrotype plates. These required no engraving and were faster, easier, and dramatically less costly. The possibility of using photographic images expanded in direct relation to this drop in costs.

Then, in the late 1880s, the rotary press virtually replaced the flatbed press. Printing speed exploded, publishing costs plummeted, magazine and newspaper circulations skyrocketed, and the extensive publication of photographs began in earnest. This development also cleared the way for the consumer magazine, which, along with newspapers, would provide a huge market for photographers that expanded almost without interruption until the advent of the Internet.

The world of photography had just blown wide open to someone who wanted

Over: Woman with bundle of sticks.

to wander great distances, record on film the lives of the people she met, and pay her own way. Within four years Edith Watson would be doing just that.

In a world where images bombard us during all our waking hours, it is probably impossible to imagine the impact of the invention of photography. Before photography, wealthy Europeans and North Americans could look at or perhaps even own paintings in their homes or palaces and see them in museums. They had (often unrealistically flattering) portraits made of themselves and their heroes, of their families and their estates, of the wars they won, and of events that mattered to them.

Ordinary people had no such access. Churches almost entirely provided—and controlled—what the public saw in paintings, frescoes, mosaics, and sculptures. These were intended to inspire faith and/or fear. They indicated a better, and sometimes worse, time and place and rarely reflected anything of the lives of the people who saw them. And they most certainly did not record the lives of those people.

Photography changed all that. The new ability to use light to fix an image on paper constituted a revolution, albeit a quiet one. It shifted how we see, imagine, remember, experience, and think about people, places, and events. Photography created images of celebrations, storms, fires, wars, mountains, seas, deserts, forests, destruction, creation, the wonders of faraway places, the animals, birds, insects, and people who make and inhabit all our worlds. Photography can share views through a microscope and images from outer space. Without photography there would be no television. No computers. No Internet. We would have a fraction of the discoveries of science and medicine that make our lives better and longer. We would have fewer images of people, families, friends, strangers, and what they do. We would have no record of any of these things through time. We would not know what the people around us looked like. We might have a small mirror or see our own face reflected in a calm pool, but we would have no further indication of what we ourselves looked like. And what about yesterday? Ten years ago? We could have our imaginings. Other than perhaps a pencil sketch we would have no visual records.

By 1890 portrait photography was available in St. John's. Richard Holloway had started taking summer excursions in the hope of improving his health, and a few prosperous Newfoundlanders owned cameras (including future professional photographer Elsie Holloway). But for most people, life was too harsh to allow money and time to take photographs.

Into this came a young woman with a camera, eager to record daily life, the people she met, the work they did, and the outports they lived in. She was prepared to wait for days to get the right conditions and combinations of light, people, and activity for her box camera with glass-plate negatives and albumen prints, and later her mail-in Kodak cameras and other Kodaks with acetate negatives. She was happy to leave photographs with the people she met and to exchange them for lodging and transportation. She liked and respected the people she met, and from the looks on their faces and the fact that they welcomed her back year after year, they enjoyed her.

Thousands of Edith's photographs appeared as advertisements or illustrations in newspapers and magazines. In the style of the day, some images mimic the European and Canadian Impressionists and their French predecessors, notably Jean François Millet (1814–75). Others range from pictorial to photojournalistic. The composition of her photographs is impeccable, even if her developing of them was not always stellar. The images are gentle and kind and made with a sense of collaboration, whether depicting back-breaking work on the fish flakes, carrying hay in quilts, or going home from the well with water pails balanced on hoops.

Photography, like other arts, is a dance, an interplay, of creator, seer, seen, and for published photographs, the context in which they appear. Once a photograph goes out into the world, its image is set, finished. What remains dynamic, different with each viewer and each viewing, is the interpretation.

· · ·

"Uncle Tom" and "Fovey"
on board the schooner
"Nilton", from Tippers
Harbor, to the French
shore at "La Scie".
Aug. 22nd.

Along the shore, at Hermitage.

My introduction to Edith Watson's Canadian albums was in a corner of a second-floor bedroom. A pile of books, including the albums, had cascaded from a collapsed bookcase under a leaking roof. Several books were damp, but the albums were dry and whole. Lois Watson and I pulled them out and moved them to a table in the next room. The books were those written by Edith and Amelia's friends and colleagues. Amelia had provided watercolours for some, Edith photographs for others. Lois and I organized them against the wall opposite the dripping ceiling. Then, finally, I opened the albums.

The albums themselves are nothing special. Most of them are the 12-by-14.5-inch kind of scrapbook that Woolworth's sold for decades. That they are so unprepossessing from the outside only increases the surprise and thrill of discovering their contents. A title appears on the inside front cover of each book: "A Story of Fish … in

The home-made pieced bed quilt often comes in handy for bringing in the hay in the Newfoundland out-ports where horses are unknown. In Hermitage.

Women ashore all along the Newfoundland coast lend a hand at the fish, leaving their men free to go to their fishing, in Petty Harbour.

Pictures as seen by Edith S. Watson and Victoria Hayward the Writer, in their many voyages through Canada, Newfoundland, and the French Islands of St. Pierre and Miquelon"; "Children from Here and There in Canada [and] Newfoundland"; "Banff and Lake Louise"; "The Way of the Wells ... from Canada to Newfoundland"; "Alert Bay"; "Delightful Visits among the Doukhobors"; "Quebec"; "New Canadians"; and finally: "Happy Souvenirs of trips made alone to Newfoundland and to Labrador in

On the marsh, Cape Ray.

Company with Miss Victoria Hayward, the Writer."

    Going through the albums one by one and page by page, I could hardly believe what I was seeing. Women. Working. Hard. Smiling, scowling, some posing, some paying no attention to the camera. An invitation to a different world. Even now, more than half a lifetime later, these images give me goosebumps. I never tire of looking. There is always something fresh, something to discover. I never see the body of work or the individual images the same way twice: a child looks more tender or eager, a woman more energetic or tired, a man more at ease or careworn, a place more difficult to wrench a fresh vegetable from or more inviting than ever before. Emily Carr wrote in her journal, "Something of you can get trapped forever in the picture as long as it lasts." Given my journey with Edith and her work, I would suggest that something of the picture can get trapped in you as long as you last.

An identifying caption or penciled note on the back of most of the photographs provides a snippet of information. The majority of these notes are in Edith's writing, some in Queenie's. Frustratingly, almost none of the photographs are dated. The latest date I have found is on a print from Newfoundland in 1929, almost 40 years after the first shots, and certainly indicating a spread of time she spent in no other area.

The albums, along with Edith's credited published photographs, provide a rich showing of her work. What about the rest, the ones she gave to friends and left with families along her way? What about the anonymous 7-by-9, 4-by-4, and 2-by-2-inch prints, the prints on family mantelpieces and dressers, in albums, attics, and envelopes marked "what are these?" and stuck in an old book? How to tell if a photograph is one of Edith's?

With luck, she will have written on the back of a print and used her "Edith S. Watson, East Windsor Hill, Ct" stamp. Otherwise, composition and subjects distinguish her work. Rural settings with women, children, men, farm animals and birds (especially geese) portrayed with gentle dignity. Some, not many, landscapes. Ships. Figureheads. Country laneways. Simple scenes. She frequently uses diagonals to enhance perspective and depth. People tend to be at the centre of the photographs, not used as props for some other focus. While many of her photographs are posed, none are prettified, none indicate a greater status for one person over another or others.

An example: A woman sent me a photograph taken in Gaultois early in the 20th century. She wondered if it might be one of Edith's. It shows flakes and a newly constructed building with men standing mid-photograph and part of a group of women to the far left.

My first question: Is this print made from the entire negative? If it is, this is not one of Edith's. Under no circumstances would she cut off the women and put the

Drying cod, Petty Harbour, where I boarded with Mrs. Mary Hannaford.

men front and centre. It is unlikely but not impossible that she would put buildings as the central image. If the original negative is available, it would be possible to see whether the print is cropped. Edith would not willingly have cropped a negative this way, so she did not develop this print. She would have focused on the women and left out much of the rest. If someone else used the negative to print this image, then the original image could be hers. She would never have approved this use of it.

Whatever the intent of the creator, an image will speak to each viewer in the way that person most needs at the time. The people to whom I've showed Edith's photographs are no exception. A prominent writer of children's literature looked at Edith's images of children and commented on their empathy, their artistry. A

"The cows are coming home"
In St. Joachim,
Que.

painter noted their almost-Impressionist nature. A writer, a gallery owner, and a property developer who live on the west coast all saw the uncanny similarity between Watson's coastal photographs and some of Emily Carr's paintings.

Edith's photograph of cows going over a hill in Quebec that I had always seen as a beautifully crafted, painterly scene was part of a show at the Owens Art Gallery at Mount Allison University. The rural nature of Edith's work drew many people from the area, and virtually every local farmer who saw that picture said, "Skinny cows."

A man who drove three hours to meet with me in Toronto to see Edith's Newfoundland photographs looked at two or three of them, turned his back, said, "Look how she's colonizing them. Making fun of them. Looking down on them," and stomped out. He later came back to say that he had clawed his way from terrible poverty in a tiny outport to be the first and so far only member of his family to finish high school, let alone complete a PhD and find success in the financial world. Those photographs had captured the background he both cherishes and daily denies in order to maintain the life he has built.

At a talk I gave in St. John's, one Newfoundlander shrieked with delight at seeing a well he went to as a child. Another saw the house he had just bought, a third the church where he grew up, and yet another looked at a child carrying hay in a quilt and blurted, "That's my aunt!" What will others see in these images?

Selected Bibliography

In addition to the photograph albums, the Watson materials include loose photographs, negatives, oil and watercolour paintings, hand-painted photographs, exhibition catalogues, books and pamphlets illustrated by Edith and her sister Amelia, diaries of Amelia Watson and Victoria Hayward, scrapbooks of travels, reviews, and matters of general interest to Edith, lists of sales, family letters, wills, publishers' letters and contracts, and manuscript and published versions of *Romantic Canada*.

Essential to *Working the Rock* is the huge foundation provided by the feminist research and writing of recent decades, much of which is now being lost from library and personal collections. Secondary sources listed here arise from and are made possible by that base. For some of these original works, particularly concerning late 19th- and early 20th-century women, see the bibliography in *Working Light*.

Newfoundland and Labrador is fortunate to have some remarkable primary sources, notably works like those of Elizabeth Goudie and Hilda Murray. The *Census of Newfoundland and Labrador* (1901, collections.mun.ca/cdm/ref/collections/cns_tools/id/56973; 1911, https://archive.org/details/1911981911fnfldv11914eng) provides rich and detailed information. Some of the women Rhonda Pelley and Sheilagh O'Leary interviewed in their enchanting 2010 book *Island Maid: Voices of Outport Women* were alive when Edith Watson travelled around Newfoundland.

Antler, Ellen. "Women's Work in Newfoundland Fishing Families." *Atlantis* 2, no. 2 (1977): 106–13.

Batchen, Geoffrey. *William Henry Fox Talbot*. New York: Phaidon, 2008.

Benoit, Cecilia. "Mothering in a Newfoundland Community, 1900–1940." In *Delivering Motherhood: Maternal Ideologies and Practices in the 19th and 20th Centuries*, edited by Katherine

Arnup, Andrée Levesque, and Ruth Roach Pierson, with Margaret Brennan, 173–89. London: Routledge, 1990.

Berger, John. *Understanding a Photograph*. New York: Aperture, 2013.

Buchanan, Roberta and Bryan Greene, eds., and Anne Hart, biog. *The Woman Who Mapped Labrador: The Life and Expedition Diary of Mina Hubbard*. Montreal: McGill-Queen's University Press, 2005.

Burns, Ken. *The National Parks, American's Best Idea*, Part 1. Film. PBS. 2009.

Canadian Magazine of Politics, Science, Art and Literature (title varies). 1900–1925.

Close, Susan. *Framing Identity: Social Practices of Photography in Canada (1880–1920)*. Winnipeg: Arbeiter Ring Publishing, 2007.

DeSoto, Lewis. *Emily Carr*. Toronto: Penguin, 2008.

Conrad, Margaret R. and James K. Hiller. *Atlantic Canada: A History*. Don Mills, ON: Oxford, 2010.

Doran, Barbara and Natalie Dubois, producers. *Newfoundland at Armageddon.* Film. CBC Documentaries. 2016.

Duley, Margot Iris. "Documents: Women's Suffrage." In *Pursuing Equality: Historical Perspectives on Women in Newfoundland and Labrador,* edited by Linda Kealey, 222–29. St. John's: Institute of Social and Economic Research, Memorial University of Newfoundland (ISER), 1993.

Eastman Kodak. *How to Make Good Pictures*. Canadian ed. Toronto, 1919.

Eastman Kodak. *International Glossary of Photographic Terms*. Rochester: Eastman Kodak Company, 1973.

Fox Talbot, William Henry. *The Pencil of Nature*. Introduction by Beaumont Newhall. London: Longman, Brown, Green, & Longmans, Paternoster Row, 1844; New York: Da Capo, 1969.

Fox Talbot, Henry. *Selected Texts and Bibliography*. Edited by Mike Weaver. Oxford: Cleo Press, 1992.

Gibson, Sally. *Inside Toronto: Urban Interiors 1880s to 1920s.* Toronto: Cormorant, 2006.

Goldberg, Vicki. *Light Matters: Writings on Photography*. New York: Aperture, 2000.

Goudie, Elizabeth. *Woman of Labrador*. Edited and introduction by David Zimmerly. Toronto: The Book Society of Canada, 1983.

Greenhill, Ralph and Andrew Birrell. *Canadian Photography, 1839–1920*. Toronto: Coach House, 1979.

Greenland, Cyril and John Robert Colombo, comps. *Walt Whitman's Canada*. Toronto: Hounslow, 1992.

Hayward, Victoria, text, and Edith S. Watson, photos. *Romantic Canada*. Toronto: Macmillan, 1922.

Heritage Newfoundland. Thumbnail sketches of Newfoundland and Labrador history. www.heritage.nf.ca.

Holloway, Richard. *Through Newfoundland with the Camera*. Edited by Elsie Holloway and Bert Holloway. Rev. ed. London: Sach and Co., 1910.

Jamieson, Scott and Anne Thareau, trans. and eds. 2013. *French Visitors to Newfoundland*. St. John's: ISER, 2013.

Jones, Laura. *Rediscovery: Canadian Women Photographers, 1841–1941*. Exhibition catalogue. London, ON: London Regional Art Gallery, 1983.

Jones, Laura. "Rediscovery: Canadian Women Photographers, 1841–1941." Talk to the Photographic Historical Society of Canada, Toronto, April 19, 2006.

Kealey, Linda, ed. *Pursuing Equality: Historical Perspectives on Women in Newfoundland and Labrador*. St. John's: ISER, 1993.

Keough, Willeen G. *The Slender Thread: Irish Women on the Southern Avalon, 1750–1860*. New York: Columbia University Press, 2009. www.gutenberg-e.org.

Kennedy, John C., ed. *History and Renewal of Labrador's Inuit-Metis*. St. John's: ISER, 2014.

Kirwin, William J., George M. Story, and John D.A. Widdowson, eds. *Dictionary of Newfoundland English*. Toronto: University of Toronto Press, 1990.

Knight, Katherine and David Craig, producers. *Strange and Familiar: Architecture on Fogo Island*. Film. Site Media. 2015.

Koltun, Lily, ed. *Private Realms of Light: Amateur Photography in Canada, 1839–1940*. Markham, ON: Fitzhenry and Whiteside, 1984.

Macmillan Company of Canada (Hugh Eayrs). *A Canadian Publishing House*. Toronto: Macmillan, 1923.

Mannion, John J., ed. *The Peopling of Newfoundland: Essays in Historical Geography*. St. John's: ISER, 1977.

McGrath, Antonia. *Newfoundland Photography 1849–1949*. St. John's: Breakwater, 1980.

McGrath, Carmelita, Barbara Neis, and Marilyn Porter, eds. *Their Lives and Times: Women in Newfoundland and Labrador: A Collage*. St. John's: Killick, 1995.

Morley, Margaret Warner. *Down North and Up Along*. Illustrations from photographs by Amelia Watson, Edith S. Watson, and Frank G. Warner. New York: Dodd Mead, 1900.

Mortimer-Lamb, Harold. "Photography as a Means of Artistic Expression." *Canadian Magazine of Politics, Science, Art and Literature* 39 (May 1913): 35–46.

Murray, Hilda Chaulk. *More than 50%. Woman's Life in a Newfoundland Outport 1900–1950*. St. John's: Breakwater, 1979.

Murray, Hilda Chaulk. *Cows Don't Know It's Sunday: Agricultural Life in St. John's*. St. John's: ISER, 2002.

Nadel-Klein, Jane and Dona Lee Davis, eds. *To Work and to Weep: Women in Fishing Economies*. St. John's: ISER, 1988.

Newhall, Beaumont. *The History of Photography from 1839 to the Present Day*. Rev. ed. New York: Museum of Modern Art, 1982.

Panofsky, Ruth. *The Literary Legacy of the Macmillan Company of Canada.* Toronto: University of Toronto Press, 2012.

Pelley, Rhonda, text, and Sheilagh O'Leary, photos. *Island Maid: Voices of Outport Women*. St. John's: Breakwater, 2010.

Porter, Marilyn. "'The Tangly Bunch': Outport Women of the Avalon Peninsula." *Newfoundland Studies* 1, no. 1 (1985): 77–90.

Queller, Georgina Olivere, Roberta Buchanan, and Geraldine Chafe Rubia, eds. *A Charm against the Pain*. St. John's: Pennywell Books, 2006.

Rooney, Frances. "Finding Edith S. Watson." *Blatant Image* 1 (1981): 86.

Rooney, Frances. "Edith S. Watson, Photographer, and Victoria Hayward, Writer." *Fireweed* 13 (1982): 60–68.

Rooney, Frances. "Finding Edith Watson." *Resources for Feminist Research* 12, no. 1 (1983): 26–28.

Rooney, Frances. "Edith S. Watson: A Photoessay." *Canadian Woman Studies* 7, no. 3 (1986): 48–49.

Rooney, Frances. *Edith S. Watson: Rural Canadians at Work, 1890–1920*. Exhibition catalogue. Sackville, NB: Owens Art Gallery, 1991.

Rooney, Frances. "My Dear, Dear Edith." Exhibition brochure. Galiano Island: Nuse Gallery, 1994.

Rooney, Frances. "Edith S. Watson: Photographing Women in Rural Canada." *International Journal of Canadian Studies* 11 (Spring 1995): 185–94.

Rooney, Frances. *Working Light: The Wandering Life of Photographer Edith S. Watson*. Ottawa: Carleton University Press/McGill-Queen's University Press and Images Publishing (Malvern) UK, 1996.

Rooney, Frances. "Photographer: Edith Watson." 1997. coolwomen.ca.

Rooney, Frances. "Edith S. Watson and Victoria Hayward." In *Extraordinary Women Explorers*, by Frances Rooney, 29–38. Toronto: Second Story Press, 2005.

Taft, Robert. *Photography and the American Scene, A Social History, 1839–1889*. New York: Macmillan, 1938.

Thornton, Patricia. "The Problem of Out-Migration from Atlantic Canada, 1871–1921." *Acadiensis* 15, no. 1 (1985): 3–34.

Ward, Peter. *A History of Domestic Space: Privacy and the Canadian Home*. Vancouver and Toronto: UBC Press, 1999.

White, Marian Frances. *The Finest Kind: Voices of Newfoundland and Labrador Women*. St. John's: Creative, 1997.

Acknowledgements

As with all my work around Edith Watson, three people other than Edith herself have been crucial: Frieda Forman, who showed me that first photograph and suggested, "Why don't you see if you can find more of her work?" the woman in the Smithsonian who made it possible to find Edith's family, and Lois Watson. Lois recognized that Edith's work was special and preserved it. Without her, none of what you see and read here would exist. Lois changed me; she enlarged and enriched my life. She did the same for Canadian social and photographic history. She was an extraordinary friend.

Librarians and archivists are a special breed. My deep thanks to the literally hundreds of them who, from the beginning, have helped find Edith and then fill in her story. In the last year I have been especially fortunate to enjoy a space in the Writers' Room of the Toronto Reference Library. With little or often no talk at all, the staff and other writers there provide a context that affirms and supports us in a way that writers desperately need.

David Quinton has for years been a friend and advocate for Edith and me. When we met, I had no idea that he was the longtime producer and host of *Land and Sea* as well as a filmmaker. He phoned and said that he'd found *Working Light* in a grocery-store book section and loved it. We went from there. He and

Françoise provide warmth from St. John's in all weathers and I'm delighted that he is now also the author of two books.

Among others also in St. John's are longtime friends Joan Scott and Helen Porter. St. John's transplant journalist Cynthia Long, who now lives not far from me, provided useful insights and information.

In Toronto, Sally Gibson, historian, archivist, and author of dazzling books about Toronto heritage, needs particular notice. During the writing of this book, and despite major difficulties, she has provided unwavering support. Steven Evans, photographer and collector, has provided much information, encouragement, and delightful conversation. In my darkest time, his plain speaking kept me from giving up on this book. He and Sally both read and made suggestions concerning the manuscript. Author and storyteller extraordinaire Celia Barker Lottridge, too, has offered support and suggestions. Also needing mention here are photographers Susan Staton and Rolando Mei and curator and source of light Emily McKibbon.

This book was launched by the answer to every writer's dream: a cold call from a publisher, in this case Gavin Will, asking, "Would you be interested in writing another book about Edith Watson?" *Would I?* Since then, staff editor Stephanie Porter and I have done our best to navigate some utterly unexpected and pretty rough waters.

My thanks to them and to Elsa Flack, who suggested this book to Gavin and almost talked me into buying an outport house.

Finally, partner Deanna Derksen kept me warm, happy, laughing—and going. She never once complained about all the time and attention I gave to Edith. And especially during the last three months, when I've been able to do nothing, she has kept me alive, fed, and loved. Life in our house has been and will again be very sweet.

Frances Rooney's books include *Working Light: The Wandering Life of Photographer Edith S. Watson* (published in Canada, the US, and Britain), *Our Lives* (finalist for the Lambda Award), and two books for the Women's Hall of Fame Series—*Extraordinary Women Explorers* and *Exceptional Women Environmentalists*. She and her partner live in a house overlooking the woods, raccoons, squirrels, birds, deer, and coyotes in a Toronto ravine.